LET'S TALK ABOUT

Stepfamilies

Sarah Levete

Stargazer Books

© **Aladdin Books Ltd 2006**

Designed and produced by
Aladdin Books Ltd

**First published in the
United States in 2006 by**
Stargazer Books
c/o The Creative Company
123 South Broad Street
P.O. Box 227
Mankato, Minnesota 56002

Printed in Malaysia

Design: Flick, Book Design
and Graphics
Picture Research:
Brian Hunter Smart
Editors:
Jim Pipe & Rebecca Pash

The consultant, Vicky Leach, is
Family Mediation & Children's
Support Services Adviser for the
children's charity NCH.

The photographs reproduced in
this book have been posed by
models or have been obtained
from photographic agencies.

*Library of Congress Cataloging- in-
Publication Data*

Levete, Sarah.
  Stepfamilies / by Sarah Levete.
    p. cm. -- (Let's talk about)
  Includes index.
  ISBN 1-59604-048-3
  1. Stepfamilies--Juvenile
  literature. I. Title. II. Let's talk
  about (Stargazer Books)

HQ759.92.L45 2005
306.874--dc22
                    2004064983

Contents

"What is a stepfamily?"

What is your family like? Do you have lots of sisters and brothers? Perhaps your family is just you and one of your parents. Some children live with their grandparents.

You may be part of a stepfamily, or you may know someone who is part of a stepfamily. All families are different and a stepfamily is just one type of family.

A stepfamily is just one type of family.

A stepfamily is formed when one parent meets a new partner. They might live together or get married. One or both of them may already have children.

This book helps you to understand what it means to be part of a stepfamily. It discusses how a child may feel when a stepfamily is formed. It talks about the challenges and rewards of being part of a stepfamily.

You may live in a stepfamily, or maybe someone in your class is part of a stepfamily.

"How does a stepfamily come together?"

Families change when there is a loss or a break-up. The loss may be the death of one parent. A break-up happens if parents decide to live apart.

When this happens, one or both parents may meet another partner and live with him or her. This creates a stepfamily.

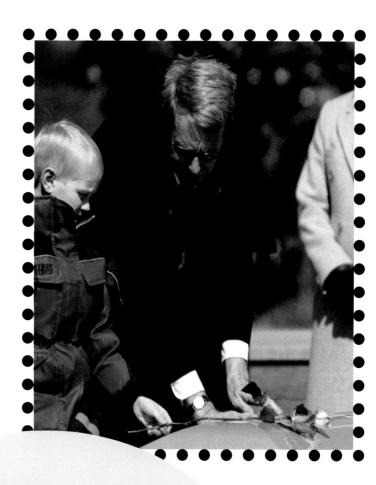

A stepfamily can form after a parent dies and the other parent meets a new partner.

It's important to remember that whatever the reason for parents being apart, it is never a child's fault.

Children who form part of a stepfamily will have been part of another family, their first family. Babies or young children may be part of a stepfamily. Others may become part of a stepfamily as teenagers.

Did you know…

There are different kinds of parents. The mom and dad who made you are biological or birth parents. They may also be called blood parents.

Whatever happens, they will always be your birth parents. Some children, who also have stepparents, call their birth parents their "real" or "natural" mom and dad.

"What's a step-family like?"

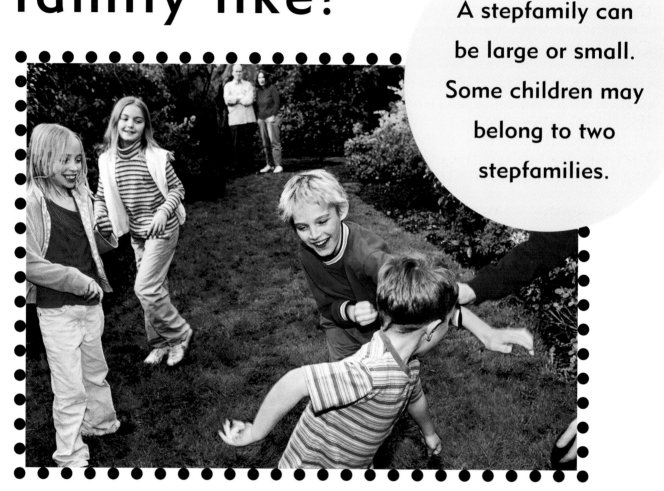

A stepfamily can be large or small. Some children may belong to two stepfamilies.

Just like any other family, stepfamilies come in all shapes and sizes. In some stepfamilies, the birth and stepparent may be of the same sex. Some parents marry, and others decide simply to live together.

A stepfamily may be made up of one child and the birth and stepparent. Or, if your stepparent has his or her own children, these become your step-brothers and -sisters.

If the birth and stepparent have a baby together, this is your halfbrother or -sister.

If both birth parents set up home with new partners, you may find yourself with two stepfamilies!

Don't forget, you'll also have two new sets of aunts, uncles, and grandparents. It can get quite complicated!

Think about it

If your birth and stepparent have a baby together, you may worry that it will stop you from being special. But nothing is likely to change your parents' love for you. Talking to both your birth and stepparent can reassure you. And having a baby brother or sister can be fun!

"What happens in a stepfamily?"

When a family breaks up, for whatever reason, there are lots of confusing feelings to deal with. A stepfamily then coming together can create even more difficult feelings. There can be lots of difficult decisions to make, such as who lives with whom.

Each family situation is different. Some children are very close to and may live with their stepfamily. Others have little or no contact.

As a stepfamily comes together, there are lots of issues to deal with.

Some children can choose how much they are involved and others are given no choice. This can be hard to accept.

Explain clearly to your parents how you feel. It may not change anything, but it will help you deal with the situation.

Think about it

A stepfamily is no more or less of a family than any other type of family. But a stepfamily does face more challenges. Everyone has to adjust to the break-up of the first family and the coming together of the new family. It can be hard, but in time everyone can enjoy being part of a stepfamily.

"Do stepfamilies always live together?"

Some children live with the stepfamily for all or most of the time. This may mean moving to a new home or perhaps moving to a new school in a new area.

Other children visit the step-family at weekends. If so, it helps to feel part of the family by having a special place in the stepfamily's house for your belongings.

Some children move home to live with the stepfamily. Others visit the stepfamily occasionally.

Living with one family for half the week and the stepfamily for the rest of the week is fun, but also quite challenging!

It's not easy to organize your belongings between two houses or to remember the different household rules. Talk to your parents if you are finding it difficult.

My story

"I live with my stepfamily and see my dad on school breaks. I had to move home and change schools. At first I missed my friends but I keep in touch by email. One of my old friends is coming to stay for a weekend and I've made some new friends at school too." Charlie

"Does everything change in a stepfamily?"

Sometimes, everything in a stepfamily feels different. Your stepfamily may be from a different culture or have different religious beliefs. There may be new rules about watching TV or doing homework, or you may not be used to the food. These things can make you feel as if you don't fit in. But in time, everything will seem less strange and you will feel more relaxed.

You may not be used to the way your stepfamily does things.

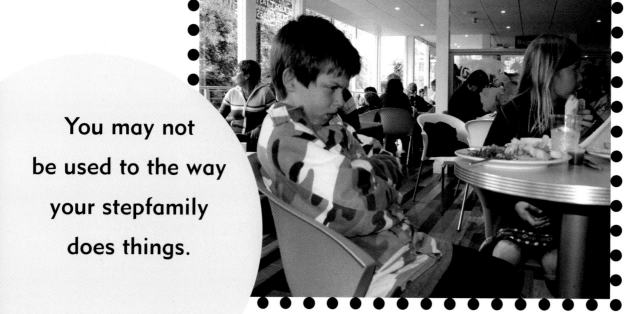

Try to show consideration and respect for any differences in your stepfamily. Tolerance and understanding will make it easier for everyone to settle in.

Adapting to change takes time. It's confusing at first, but once you have gotten used to it, change can bring good feelings too.

Think about it

Becoming part of a stepfamily doesn't change your first family's feelings toward you. They will go on loving you. And you can go on loving your birth parents and brothers and sisters, just as before.

"How does it feel to be part of a stepfamily?"

For many, becoming part of a stepfamily creates difficult feelings. Children may still be upset by the break-up of the first family or be grieving for a lost parent. It is common to feel confused or lonely.

You may feel angry toward other family members. You may think that nobody is interested in you or feel as if you don't belong. You may miss your other parent. All of these feelings are natural.

It is common to feel confused, angry, or upset. In time, these feelings pass.

It's easier to deal with feelings if you can express them. Try writing them down, or talk to your parents or close friends.

Whatever is going on at home, try not to let it affect everything else. Keep up with any activities you enjoy, such as playing with friends.

My story

"I missed Mom so much after she died. I was angry with Dad for meeting Jill, my stepmom. I didn't want a new mom. It was like I didn't belong anywhere. I used to argue with everyone. Talking to my teacher really helped. Now I tell Dad and Jill how I feel. I still miss Mom but I've accepted the situation now."
Sasha

"Do I have to like my stepparent?"

Just because your birth parent loves your stepparent, it doesn't mean you will feel the same! Try not to worry if you don't like your stepparent. It takes time to get to know anyone.

In the meantime, learn how to get along with each other as well as possible. Avoid comparing your step- and birth parent. Everyone is different and has different ways of doing things.

You may not like your stepparent at first, but try to give him or her a chance.

You may think your step-parent is trying to replace your birth parent. This is probably not the case, but your stepparent may be trying too hard to make friends with you.

Some children call their stepparent by his or her first name. Others call him or her "Dad" or "Mom." Decide with your stepparent what feels right for all of you.

Think about it

Try to show respect and kindness to your stepparent, even if you don't feel happy about the situation.

Remember, he or she may also feel anxious about getting to know you. Your stepparent may not have looked after children before, so be patient!

"What about step-brothers and -sisters?"

Just as you are joining a new family, so too may your stepbrothers and -sisters. They probably feel equally unsure and anxious!

If you are not used to sharing your parent's attention, you may feel jealous or resentful toward a new stepbrother or -sister.

Sharing your parent's attention with a stepbrother or -sister can be hard.

Yet, nothing will change the special love between you and your birth parent.

Ask your birth parent if you can spend some time alone together. If you are used to living in a quiet house with plenty of room, you may find it hard living in a noisy, crowded house.

Talk to your parents. They may not be able to magically get a big quiet house for you, but they may be able to arrange some space and quiet time for each child.

Did you know...

There's good news! Stepbrothers and -sisters can be great fun. They are ready-made new friends.

Older children can help you out with homework, and younger ones will really look up to you!

"What about my 'real' parent?"

Some children, especially those who live with the step-family most of the time, feel anxious about, and miss, their other birth parent. But remember that you can still love your mom or dad, even if you live apart.

It's natural to miss your birth parent, but this needn't stop you enjoying time with your stepfamily.

Some parents continue to argue even after separating. It is not fair if you feel caught in the middle and pressurized to take sides. Explain to your parents how this makes you feel.

Many children feel disloyal to the birth parent if they get on with the stepparent. But it's OK to love both sets of parents.

Having a good relationship with your stepparent won't stop you from loving your "real" mom or dad.

Did you know…

Some children feel relieved to be in a stepfamily, especially if their mom or dad is happier. But this can create feelings of guilt and worry about the other birth parent. Remember, you can feel happy as part of a stepfamily and still love your other family.

"Why does it take time for a stepfamily to settle?"

It takes time to adjust to a loss or break-up of parents in the first family, and to accept a new family. Some children may blame their stepparent for their parents' break-up. But this is not fair and won't help the stepfamily settle. Try to give your stepparent a chance.

There may be many ups and downs for everyone. But in time you will come to know and accept each other.

Other children may blame themselves for their parents' separation. But it is never the child's fault. Blaming yourself makes it harder to accept the new situation.

Some children behave badly, hoping to drive their step-parent away. This will make things difficult and unsettled, but it won't make the birth parents get back together.

Try to ignore negative comments from people, such as relatives. Let them know how it makes you feel and ask them not to say things that make it difficult for you.

My story

"Everything was fine until birthdays or holidays. There were arguments about who I would stay with but now my parents take turns. It's taken quite a long time to get used to having two families, but I'm beginning to enjoy it."
Ada

"How can stepfamilies resolve problems?"

Bottling up your feelings will not help! Talk to one or both of your parents, or to another person you trust. It may not change the situation, but it will help you feel better. You may find new support and friends in your stepgrandparents or relatives. And your birth grandparents will still be there for you.

Talking about problems is the first step toward solving them.

Think about it

There are lots of fairy tales with wicked stepmothers and evil stepfathers. These stories may be fun to read, but they are very unfair on real stepparents.

Being a stepparent is not easy. Remember that stepmoms and -dads try hard to fit in and feel at home with their new family.

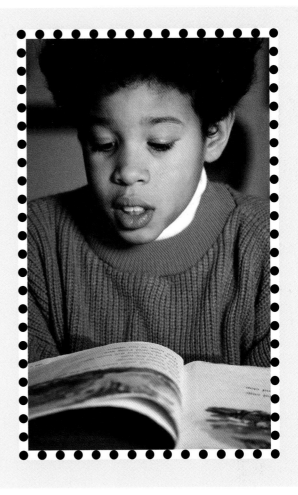

If there are problems about seeing your birth parent, tell your parents how you feel and what you would like to happen. If they are not able to agree, they can get a mediator to help figure out arrangements. If you feel left out, particularly if step relatives seem only to notice your stepbrothers or -sisters, explain how you feel. They might not be aware of how they are making you feel.

"What makes a happy stepfamily?"

There is no magic way to create an instant happy stepfamily. It takes time and patience. The tips below may help.

① Accept that there will be sad and difficult feelings about the break-up of the first family.

② Be thoughtful about other members of the stepfamily, even if you don't like them much.

③ Talk to family members about how you feel.

In time, members of a stepfamily can learn to enjoy each other's company.

④ Ask your parents for family meetings when everyone can discuss any problems, such as who chooses what to watch on TV. The family can listen to each other and try to resolve problems together.

⑤ Try to do some things together as a family so that you can share experiences and have shared memories.

Did you know...

There are lots of good things about being in a stepfamily. You'll see your birth parent in a happy relationship. You'll understand that relationships take time to develop. Your step-parent may become a good friend in whom you can confide. You'll have great experiences of new people and ways of living.

"What can I do?"

- Accept that there will be difficult feelings to deal with.
- Talk to others about how you are feeling.
- Remember that it will take time for everyone to adjust.
- Give everyone a chance to settle in. Try to be tolerant and understanding.

- Remember that just like other families, stepfamilies argue with each other and then make friends again.
- If you know another child who is finding it hard to settle in a stepfamily, why not make a special effort to include him or her in your games?

Enjoy the new experiences that a stepfamily gives you.

Books on stepfamilies

If you want to read more about stepfamilies, try:

How Do I Feel About My Stepfamily by Julie Johnson (Stargazer)

On the Web

These websites are also helpful:

www.womenandchildren.org

www.kids-right.org

www.jointcustody.org

www.bbbsa.org

Contact information

If you want to talk to someone who doesn't know you, these organizations can help:

Active Parenting
1955 Vaughn Road NW
Suite 108
Kennesaw
GA 30144-7808
www.activeparenting.com

Children's Rights Council
220 Eye Street, NE
Washington, DC 20002
(202) 547-6227
www.gocrc.com

Stepfamily
Association of
America
215 Centennial
 Mall South
Suite 212
Lincoln, NE 68508
(402) 477-7837
www.saafamilies.org

Stepfamily Foundation
333 West End Avenue
New York, NY 10023
(212) 877-3244
www.stepfamily.org

There is lots of useful information about families on the internet.

Index

Photocredits

Abbreviations: l-left, r-right, b-bottom, t-top, c-center, m-middle
All photos supplied by Digital Vision except for:
3tr, 5b, 9b, 27t — Photodisc. 6r — Shane T McCoy/US Navy. 7b — John E Woods/US Navy. 10, 14b, 16b, 18b, 25br — PBD. 13bl — Brand X Pictures. 17tl — Corbis. 22b, 24b, 26b — Jim Pipe.